AF490251

THE ORIGIN OF CORN SNAKE

Corn snakes are a very typically saved puppy snake initially from the southern states in the USA. They have been given their call because they had been typically discovered hunting mice in corn stores. They are taken into consideration harmless to people and have a totally crucial position in controlling rodent populations particularly round farms.

Corn snakes are in all likelihood the most famous puppy snake in the UK and have been kept and bred for many years. Originally they have been red/orange and brown however they have got when you consider that been selectively bred for various pattern and coloration combinations. While they can get quite lengthy they continue to be slim and easy to handle. They generally have a totally passive attitude making them a high-quality preference

HOW TO HOUSE CORN SNAKE

Corn snakes come from a warm surroundings so they conflict with the bloodless and humidity of the UK. To insulate against each of these elements we advise retaining the snake in a wood vivarium. Due to the temperature gradient required we might generally pick an enclosure not less than three x 2 x 2ft with massive vents and glass sliding front doorways.

All of this air flow has to make certain that heat and humidity is misplaced from one facet of the enclosure to the other whilst retaining the basking spot itself at a steady temperature.

Corn snakes can be a bit shy when they are young. We still use the whole length enclosure to make certain that the suitable temperature gradient is in vicinity however we will offer greater decorations first of all.

CORN SNAKE HEATING

Naturally, corn snakes might be experiencing temperatures of round 90of within the sun. We try to offer this warmth over 1/3 of the enclosure even as letting the rest of the enclosure cool to 70of on the opposite aspect. To gain this we connect a basking lamp to the ceiling of the enclosure on one side. This is controlled by using a dimming thermostat to ensure that the temperature is saved correct for the duration of the day. Corn snakes may be able to attain the top in their enclosure without decorations to climb on so the basking lamp need to be surrounded through a defend. The basking lamp is left on for 10-12 hours consistent with day.

At night, all of the lighting fixtures must go off and the enclosure must be completely dark. This must make certain that the snake has a clean day night time cycle.

Though at this point the sun has long gone down, there might nevertheless be rocks, paths and roads which have warmed up within the day and as a way to radiate heat for plenty of the night. To offer this warmth at some point of the night time without introducing mild to the enclosure we lay a warmth mat below the basking vicinity. The warmth mat will warm objects around it imparting a warm patch of ground for the corn snake to rest on. To ensure that the heat mat remains the right temperature it is controlled by means of a easy on/off thermostat set to 80of. The warmness mat is buried underneath round an inch of bedding, the sensor for the thermostat is then rested at the bedding masking the warmth mat in order that it could tune the surface temperature of that patch of floor.

During the day your temperatures might be a good deal too heat and the ceramic lamps thermostat must hold it off automatically. The warmth mat will handiest start to heat as soon as the temperatures have dropped below 80of at night time.

Though the thermostats we sell are very dependable it's miles constantly great exercise to reveal your temperatures with a thermometer. A 5of variance on the basking spot is not anything to fear approximately as long as your cool aspect is still cool. SA simple dial thermometer on each aspect has to be sufficient but digital probe thermometers are a great deal more accurate

UVB LIGHTING FOR CORN SNAKES

Corn snakes do no longer require UVB to use the calcium in their weight loss plan like other reptiles however it's miles nevertheless a beneficial addition to the enclosure. The snake might clearly be exposed to UV from sunlight within the wild and as we're looking to emulate nature in our enclosures we endorse providing some UVB.

A 5% T8 UVB tube, 2-five% T5 uvb tube or more effective however smaller unit should be sufficient. The UV tube should be established to the ceiling at the back of the enclosure to offer a mild gradient walking parallel to the temperature gradient. There could be instances whilst the snake will need less or no UVB so partial and full hiding spots must be located all along the width of the enclosure.

HOW TO DECORATE CORN SNAKE

Corn snakes thrive in a low humidity environment with hard decorations to climb over and bask on. When deciding on bedding we strive to make sure that the pieces are not likely to boom the enclosures humidity. In shop we typically use a coarse beech woodchip as it is smooth, cheap, and smooth to identify smooth and dirt unfastened. If you select a more natural searching ornament a soil / clay blend might be best. If you intend to hold the snake in a bio-lively enclosure a nutrient rich soil and clay blend with a few sand for aeration could be perfect.

Corn snakes love the warmth coming from their basking lamp but additionally they appreciate secondary belly heat as a way to radiate from heat objects. Natural rocks like slate are best for this, so are heavy artificial ornaments. These decorations can be located underneath and across the basking place and should heat up well. If the lamp is too low there may be a hazard that herbal rocks may want to get too hot so that you are quality to check the floor temperature to keep away from burns.

As discussed inside the lighting section there can be instances whilst the snake does no longer want any UV and wishes a chunk of color. To make certain that the snake can break out from the light every time necessary we suggest spreading full and partial cowl during the enclosure. Examples of complete cowl decorations might be caves, flat cork portions or some other decoration that gives a shady spot to rest. Examples of partial cowl might encompass tall plant life, trailing flora.

FOOD FOR CORN SNAKE

Corn snakes are carnivorous and ought to be fed frozen thawed ingredients. Though they're opportunists we've got discovered that mice are the best diet for a corn snake. A specially large corn snake can also move directly to the smaller rats whilst fully grown however an all rodent food plan is quality.

As hatchlings, corn snakes should be fed weekly on defrosted pinky mice, because the snake grows the food size ought to be increased until the snake is taking massive mice or maybe jumbos. Adult corn snakes may be fed as soon as each two weeks as they are able to emerge as obese if fed weekly.

More exceptional alternative diets like gerbils, hamsters, multimammate mice or chicks could be used if the corn snake won't take anything else but they aren't as nutritious as the mice, it is able to be difficult to discover them inside the size required and they aren't always as available.

We constantly consist of a medium or big sized water bowl in the snake's enclosure. You may word the snake use it for bathing, which is typically to calm down or to help loosen its losing skin. Both the water bowl must be kept at the cool aspect of the enclosure to prevent it from elevating the humidity within the enclosure.

HOW TO BREED CORN SNAKE

If you keep a male and female together, they will breed. You do not need to do something to inspire this. As lengthy as they're healthy and the conditions are desirable, it'll happen obviously. You need to recall whether you want this to occur before introducing the pair. What will you do with the babies if you incubate the eggs?

A gravid female ought to have access to a nesting box to put her eggs. The container have to be huge sufficient that she can completely flip-around inside it.

Inside the nesting box we use a soil mix that is saved humid enough to preserve its form but not so moist that it's going to saturate any eggs. We have observed that Proper spider existence is best for this.

Once laid, the eggs must be incubated in an incubator at 84oF. We incubate our eggs in sealed bins on a moisture wealthy substrate (consisting of Hatchrite) to trap the humidity across the eggs. After about 60 days the eggs will begin to hatch, the primary infants to emerge will inspire the rest of the eggs to hatch.

HOW TO CLEAN YOUR CORN SNAKE

Corn snakes, as with most pets, require smooth surroundings to thrive. We endorse a spot clean as frequently as possible (every day) and a full clean each 4 weeks or so. If you are preserving the snake in a bio-lively enclosure you may spot smooth and display the enclosure. It may additionally nevertheless be a good object to change out the bedding some times in line with 12 months.

When cleansing the enclosure you have to eliminate your animal, all decorations and all of the bedding. Once the enclosure is clear you could spray it throughout with a reptile friendly disinfectant. These usually work very quickly and best want to be left for around 30 seconds, commands can typically be determined on the disinfectants packaging. Once the disinfectant has finished its work it may be wiped away from the surfaces with a paper towel. In some instances you would possibly need to repeat this process a 2nd time to make certain that the enclosure is thoroughly wiped clean.

Your decorations may be wiped clean in a similar technique, virtually spray them down with the disinfectant and rinse thoroughly with water before drying them off and setting them again into the enclosure. We suggest this procedure is performed all through the day time to make certain that the snake will be going back to a warm vivarium for as a minimum an hour earlier than the basking lamps are became off for the night time.

THE END

9 798844 173950